MIDDLE EAST LEADERS™

YASSER ARAFAT

Bernadette Brexel

The Rosen Publishing Group, Inc.,
New York

Published in 2004 by The Rosen Publishing Group, Inc.
29 East 21st Street, New York, NY 10010

Library of Congress Cataloging-in-Publication Data

Brexel, Bernadette.
Yasser Arafat/ by Bernadette Brexel.
    p. cm. — (Middle East Leaders)
Summary: Examines the life and leadership skills of Palestinian National Authority president Yasser Arafat, who won a Nobel Peace Prize for his efforts to establish peace in the Middle East.
Includes bibliographical references and index.
ISBN 0-8239-4469-7
1. Arafat, Yasir, 1929–—Juvenile literature. 2. Munazzamat al-Tahrir al-Filastiniyah—Presidents—Biography—Juvenile literature. 3. Palestinian Arabs—Biography—Juvenile literature. 4. Palestinian National Authority. [1. Arafat, Yasir, 1929– 2. Palestinian Arabs—Biography. 3. Palestinian National Authority. 4. Nobel Prizes—Biography.] I. Title. II. Series.
DS126.6.A67C44 2003
956.95'3044'092—dc21

                                                    2003009400

Manufactured in the United States of America

CONTENTS

INTRODUCTION

THE TWO SIDES OF ARAFAT

■ An Israeli tank lies in wait at Arafat's compound in Ramallah. Ramallah is a small town in the West Bank, handed to Palestinians in 1994 under the Oslo Accords. The Palestinian Authority used Ramallah as its center of government for the West Bank.

It's March 29, 2002, in Ramallah, in the West Bank of Israel. Helicopters hover above dozens of rolling tanks as the Israeli Defense Force (IDF) enters Ramallah. The IDF is following orders to isolate the "enemy" by raiding his compound. The order was given after the Israeli government held an all-night emergency meeting. The meeting was called because of terrorist attacks against Israeli civilians. The IDF believed that the attacks came from a military group linked to the PLO (Palestine Liberation Organization). The leader of the PLO is Yasser Arafat. If Arafat could be contained, the Israeli government thought, then maybe Arafat would call on militants to stop their terrorist attacks.

The recent terror attacks had been deadly. A suicide bomber killed twenty-two Israelis during Passover dinner in Netanya. Two elderly Israeli men in Netzarim were stabbed to death while walking to a synagogue for morning prayers. An eight-year-old Israeli boy was stabbed in an attack near his home in Elon Moreh.

"All this happened at a time when Israel's hand was—and still is—extended towards peace," the prime minister of Israel, Ariel Sharon, told the press.

IDF tanks head for Arafat's compound, the Mukata. Israeli bulldozers demolish fences and walls around the compound. Heavy machine-gun fire is exchanged between the compound guards and the attacking IDF. IDF tanks fire at the buildings, demolishing several walls and rooms. Somewhere within the compound is Arafat.

The Israeli government claims that Arafat supports terrorist attacks against Israel. It claims the PLO pays or commands the terrorists to harm Israeli citizens. The IDF plans now to cut the PLO leader off from his terrorist groups. Arafat called press organizations, such as Al-Jazeera Television, just before and during the raid on his compound and told them over the telephone, "They want to kill me,

■ Yasser Arafat concentrates on the situation at hand with his adviser, Nabil Abu-Rudaineh. Arafat and his aides were confined to a small area in a building in his compound. Arafat used his mobile phone to contact his allies for help and advice.

capture me, or expel me. I hope I will be a martyr in the Holy Land. I have chosen this path . . ."

A martyr is someone who dies for a cause. Arafat was ready to die at the hands of the IDF. According to IDF officials, the order was to isolate—not kill—Arafat. Either way, Arafat was ready to die for his cause.

Arafat's cause is Palestine and the liberation of the Palestinian people from refugee camps in Israel and surrounding Arab nations. Palestinians are mostly Arab Muslims. Arafat has fought for this cause for most of his life. Arafat began his political career in the 1950s. He wanted to establish the state of Palestine on lands where Israel had been established in 1948. He wanted a national home for the Palestinian people.

Since 1959, Arafat has fought to establish Palestinian statehood through both violent and peaceful means. Through these many years, Arafat has made certain promises to Israel and the world. He has promised that he will work to stop terrorist attacks against Israel and its Jewish citizens. He has also promised to recognize that Israel has a right to exist. Arafat has made good on the second

Arafat converses with Ahmed Yassin, the founder of Hamas, a Palestinian liberation movement. Hamas cemented its active political status in 1987 and has been declared a terrorist organization by both Israel and the United States. Hamas receives the majority of its funding from private Palestinian, Saudi, and Iranian benefactors. There is also a sprinkling of support for the group in Europe and North America.

promise, that much is fact. He has claimed to have worked to stop terror attacks as well. This claim is subject to debate.

During the 2002 Ramallah attacks, IDF officials reportedly found secret papers in Arafat's bulldozed compound during the raid. These officials claim the papers show that Arafat has given money or aid to terrorist groups. These groups have publicly waged war on Israel. They believe—as Arafat once did—that Israel shouldn't exist.

So who is right? Is Arafat a terrorist, and was Israel correct by sending the IDF to contain him? Or is Israel wrong to attack the PLO leader who has worked tirelessly for Palestinian liberation and statehood for more than forty years? It depends on whom you talk to. Many Palestinians and other Arafat supporters say his work and struggles have been just. They say he has used violence when necessary, and peace when available. Arafat's opponents and detractors have always maintained that Arafat is a terrorist who does not want peace but the destruction of Israel. The truth may lie somewhere in between these two views.

If Arafat is directly responsible for continued terrorist attacks on Israel, it means that Arafat is not the man of peace that he and his supporters have claimed for almost thirty years. The Israeli government has said it is willing to work with peaceful leaders of the Palestinian cause. It is not willing to work with terrorists, which Arafat has been accused of being and supporting.

The story of Yasser Arafat is an interesting tale. As we learn about his story, we will see that he is a man of contradictions. While some people see him as a terrorist, others see him as a hero. While some people see him as a liar and traitor, others see him as a symbol of peace and hope. Even today, the seventy-five-year-old Arafat is talking peace while terror goes on.

CHAPTER ONE

ARAFAT IN YOUTH

■ The skyline of Cairo is studded with both modern and medieval mosques that tower over the horizon. They are a symbol of the city's historical as well as present-day importance.

I t seems fitting that the man of many contradictions should have different yet "official" stories about his birth. The Palestinian Authority officially lists Old City, Jerusalem, as Yasser Arafat's birthplace. Arafat has also personally told many people that he was born in Jerusalem. According to the author of *The Mystery of Arafat*, Danny Rubinstein, Arafat has also said that he was born in Gaza, which is in the Palestinian region. Some accounts say that he was born in other Palestinian cities, such as Nablus, Safed, Lydda, and Acre.

The most widely accepted birthplace for Arafat is Cairo, Egypt. French biographers Christophe Boltanski and Jihan El-Tahri, authors of *Les sept vies de Yasser Arafat* (The Seven Lives of Yasser Arafat), have viewed his official birth certificate. It lists Cairo as his place of birth. Arafat's registration records from college also show his birthplace to be Cairo. It says that he was born on August 4, 1929. Members of his family and childhood friends have also said that Arafat was born in Cairo.

When questioned about this evidence, Arafat's usual reply is that he was born in Jerusalem, not Cairo. Arafat and others have said that his family changed the birthplace information so that Arafat would have an easier time getting into the Egyptian school system. Most sources, however, accept that Yasser Arafat was born on August 4, 1929, in Cairo.

You might be wondering why there are different stories about Arafat's birthplace. This largely has to do with Arafat's support of the Palestinian cause. If he was born in Jerusalem, then that makes him a natural Palestinian because he was born in the region of Palestine. If he was born in Egypt, then that makes him an Egyptian. Arafat learned early in his work for Palestinian liberation and statehood that Palestinians would look more favorably upon a leader who shared their ethnic identity. Arafat was shrewd in this regard.

Parents and Early Years

Arafat's father, Abdel Raouf Arafat al-Qudwa al-Husseini, was born in Gaza. He was a merchant. Arafat's mother, Zahwa Abu Saoud, was from a well-known family in Jerusalem.

Arafat's mother and father lived in Gaza and decided to move to Egypt in 1927. Yasser was born two years later. His real name is Mohammed Abdel-Raouf Arafat al-Qudwa al-Husseini. Yasser was the sixth child. Another brother was born later, making seven children in all.

Abdel Raouf's mother (Arafat's grandmother) was from an important Egyptian clan. The clan had land in Egypt. Arafat's father wanted to get the property as his inheritance. He fought in the Egyptian courts for twenty-five years but was never awarded his family's land. Arafat's father did, however, build a stable business by trading groceries, spices, and incense in Cairo.

In 1933, when Yasser was four, his mother died of kidney failure. Seven children were a lot for Abdel Raouf to manage by himself. He sent Arafat and his younger brother, Fathi, to Old City, Jerusalem. They stayed with Arafat's uncle, Selim Abu Saoud. His uncle's house was a large, comfortable place next to the Wailing Wall. This is a sacred, holy place to the Jewish people. The house was also near the al-Aqsa Mosque. The mosque is a sacred place to the Islamic people. Yasser and Fathi returned to Egypt four years later when their father remarried an Egyptian woman.

Arafat's cousin in Jerusalem remembered that Arafat always wanted to be the boss when they played together. Arafat's sister Inam also remembered that at a young age, Arafat loved to organize his playmates into military groups. He ordered them to march up and down the streets. The children wore metal plates on their heads as helmets. Arafat would hit the children with a stick when they got out of line.

Becoming Yasser

The world has come to know Mohammed Abdel-Raouf Arafat al-Qudwa al-Husseini simply as Yasser Arafat. *Yasser* means "easygoing" or "carefree" in Arabic. It is also spelled "Yasir" and "Yassir."

Yasser is a nickname that was given to Arafat at some point in his earlier years. Some sources claim that he was given his nickname when he was a child. Others, including author Danny Rubinstein, believe that he earned it in high school. Many writers, such as Andrew Gowers and Tony Walker, authors of *Behind the Myth*, believe Arafat earned his nickname while in college. It was also in college that Arafat began to find his purpose and his cause.

College and Changing Politics

Arafat applied to the University of Texas in 1948 at the age of nineteen, but he ended up at King Fouad I University in Cairo. It later became the University of Cairo. He planned to become a civil engineer.

During Arafat's first year at college, he was an average student. In fact, he had never been much of a student. Now other thoughts entered his mind. The political landscape of the region was changing. Arafat began to think about the politics of his world. He joined student groups such as the Muslim Brotherhood. He was thinking and talking about the history of the Arab people and the Middle East. What he learned quickly expanded his mind to understand the bitter history of European colonialism in the Middle East. He also saw a way to improve his own future as well as that of Palestinians and all Arabs.

The Mandated Middle East

Arafat was raised in Egypt during an important historic and political time. The world around him was changing quickly. He was raised during a time of great conflict between religions, people, rulers, and governments. A major conflict—between Britain and countries of the Middle East—had begun before Arafat was born. This conflict shaped his world and changed him forever.

The Ottomans

During the years from 1517 to 1917, the Ottoman Empire ruled the region of Palestine. The Ottomans were Islamic Turks. Palestine is one of the world's most historic areas. Its region covers part of the eastern shore of the Mediterranean Sea. At different times throughout history, it included areas of modern-day Israel, Jordan, and Egypt. Palestine has never been an independent state, however.

The people living in the Palestinian region under Ottoman rule included Arabs and Jews. The Ottoman-controlled lands included Palestine and other vast regions from the Arabian Sea to Hungary. Many Arabs lived in the Ottoman-controlled lands.

In 1914, World War I (1914–1918) started. Arafat's father was working as an officer for the Ottoman police force in Jerusalem.

■ Soldiers take cover at a drill camp in Constantinople, Turkey, in 1914. The British encouraged Arabs to fight the Turks, hoping to collapse the Ottoman Empire from within. T. E. Lawrence was perhaps the most famous military strategist involved in the operation. Lawrence organized Bedouin tribes and helped them take strategic cities under Turkish control. Lawrence later wrote a memoir based on his experiences, which was adapted to the screen in the 1962 classic film *Lawrence of Arabia*.

The Ottoman Empire joined the war on the side of Germany and Austria-Hungary. Fighting against them were the United Kingdom (Britain) and European allies such as France. The United Kingdom and the Allies hoped to win the war and conquer Ottoman lands. They planned to divide the lands into territories and states.

The Balfour Declaration

In 1917, the United Kingdom issued a special declaration stating the United Kingdom's support for the creation of a Jewish national home in Palestine.

Jews of Europe and the world would be allowed to build a Jewish state in the Palestinian region. The Jewish people would have their own government and nation.

Jews were to establish the state while respecting the various people who already lived in the region. Many of these people were Arab Muslims. Arab Muslims and Jews had lived in the region for many years without violence or hatred for one another. The declaration was meant to inspire Jews to support Britain's war efforts.

The declaration brought conflict between Arabs and Jews living inside—and outside—the Palestinian region. Arabs believed that a Jewish state could only be official so long as the Arab peoples approved it. Jews believed the declaration promised support for the Jewish Palestinian state no matter what.

Arabs living under Ottoman rule believed the war was an opportunity. If Britain and the Allies won, the Arabs would be rid of Ottoman rule. Britain encouraged Arabs to fight against the Ottomans. Britain promised that it would help the Arabs set up Arab rule in Ottoman lands if Britain won the war. In 1916, some Arabs fought against the Ottomans. Britain and the Allies won the war in 1918.

When the war ended, the League of Nations divided the Ottoman lands between Britain and France. The League of Nations was an early global political body. It was like today's United Nations. The United Nations took its place in 1946. In 1918, the divided Ottoman lands were called mandated territories. Britain and France were to help the people living in the territories set up individual governments. Other countries that fought as allies were also given mandated lands.

Britain was given mandate over Mesopotamia. Mesopotamia later became Iraq. Britain was also given mandate over Palestine, which later became Jordan and Israel. It was also given Tanganyika, in Africa, which is now part of Tanzania. France was given mandate over Syria. Syria was later divided into Syria and Lebanon.

Arabs claimed that Britain had promised Palestine to them during the war. The British had promised the Arabian leader, Hussein ibn-'Ali of Mecca, that some Ottoman lands would be made into Arab lands. Britain denied that Palestine was specifically part of the promise to the leader.

A Changing Place

The Palestinian people came from many different ethnic and religious backgrounds. The two major backgrounds were Arab and Jewish. Many of these people considered themselves "Palestinians" rather than one or the other.

During the late 1800s, a global movement formed. This movement was called Zionism. *Zion* is the poetic Hebrew word for Palestine. Zionism was the movement to build a Jewish national state in British-mandated Palestine, which is considered the ancient Jewish homeland. In 1880, there were about 24,000 Jews in Palestine. By 1914, there were more than 85,000 Jews. Jews were immigrating to Palestine by the thousands.

Jewish leaders and Zionists believed that in order to have a Jewish state, there needed to be a majority

Mandated Lands

By the early 1920s, there were more than fifteen mandated territories. The governments of Britain, France, and the other Allies were expected to watch over these territories. The League of Nations expected the governments to improve the lives of people living in mandated lands. Eventually, the territories would govern themselves and become states or countries. Other countries and their mandates included:

Belgium—Ruanda-Urundi

Japan—Islands claimed by Germany in the North Pacific Ocean

Australia—Islands claimed by Germany in Polynesia, South Pacific Ocean

New Zealand—Western Samoa (now Samoa)

Union of South Africa (South Africa)— German Southwest Africa (now Namibia)

Both United Kingdom and France— Different parts of the Cameroons and Togoland

European countries ruled over millions of square miles of foreign lands until the middle of the twentieth century.

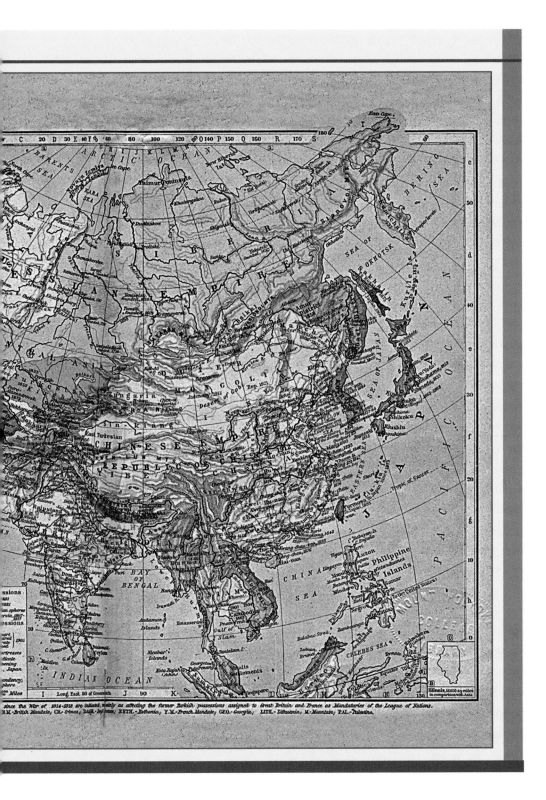

of Jewish people. Jewish leaders were happy to have Jewish immigrants pouring into Palestine. The immigrants would work hard to build up the Jewish state. It also meant that Jews all over the world would have a strong national homeland once and for all.

The rise in the Jewish population angered Arabs living in Palestine and many of the original Palestinians. They were fearful that they would lose their lands, resources, and jobs. Some Zionists were insisting that all of Palestine must become a Jewish state. The British tried to limit Jewish immigration and tried to calm the fears of those against the mass immigrations and the Zionist movement. Anti-Zionist attacks occurred nonetheless in 1920 in Jerusalem and in Jaffa in 1921.

The Nazi movement under the direction of Adolf Hitler took hold in Germany in 1933. This movement sought to eventually exterminate, or kill, the Jews of Europe and Asia. Jews by the thousands escaped by immigrating to Palestine. During 1935, 62,000 Jews entered Palestine to escape the Nazis. Arabs in Palestine continued to feel pressure from immigrating Jews. Palestinian Arabs revolted in 1936 and in 1939. The Jews and Arabs began to fight each other and Britain over Palestine.

Arafat was a mere child while this fighting was occurring, but the landscape of Palestine was drastically changing. Thousands of Palestinian Arabs left the proposed Jewish state. They went to Egypt, Jordan, Syria, and other neighboring Arab states. Unfortunately, many of these Arab states did not welcome the Palestinian Arab refugees. They treated them poorly or taxed them highly. They did very little to help their fellow Arabs.

CHAPTER TWO

RISING THROUGH THE CAUSE

■ European Jews arrive in Haifa, Palestine, in 1929. In the 1920s, approximately 100,000 Jews immigrated to Palestine. Today, Haifa is an important Palestinian port city. It is the third largest city in Israel.

As Arafat studied engineering in Cairo, fighting between Jewish and Arab Muslim groups in British-mandated Palestine was growing more violent. Britain tried to make peace, but it was impossible. Palestinian

Arabs didn't want a Jewish state. Palestinian Jews and new European Jewish immigrants did. Arafat began to make friends with Palestinian families living in Cairo. He often went to student political gatherings.

Just a year earlier, in November 1947, the United Nations made a plan to split British-mandated Palestine into two parts. One would be a Jewish state called Israel, and the other would be an Arab Muslim state called Palestine. Jerusalem—the city where Arafat's relatives lived—was to be an international city. The United Nations would control Jerusalem.

Most Jewish leaders and Palestinian Jews accepted the plan. Palestinian Arabs rejected it. Many Arab Muslims, such as Arafat, also rejected it. If a Jewish state were formed, thousands of Arab Muslims would fall under Jewish rule. Most Arab Muslims also wanted to control Jerusalem instead of allowing anyone else to. Attacks and fighting continued throughout the region.

On May 14, 1948, British control over the region came to an end. A Palestinian Jewish government had been forming. The leader, David Ben-Gurion, announced the creation of the State of Israel. Immediately, neighboring Arab states invaded Israel. The invading forces included Egypt, Iraq, Syria, Transjordan (Jordan), and Lebanon.

Even though five Arab states were warring against the newly formed country, Israel won the war. Jews call it the War of Independence. Arabs call it al-Nakbah (the Catastrophe). In 1949, the Arab states signed an agreement to end the attacks against Israel. At the end of the war, Israel controlled two-thirds of British-mandated Palestine. Israel was also accepted into the United Nations.

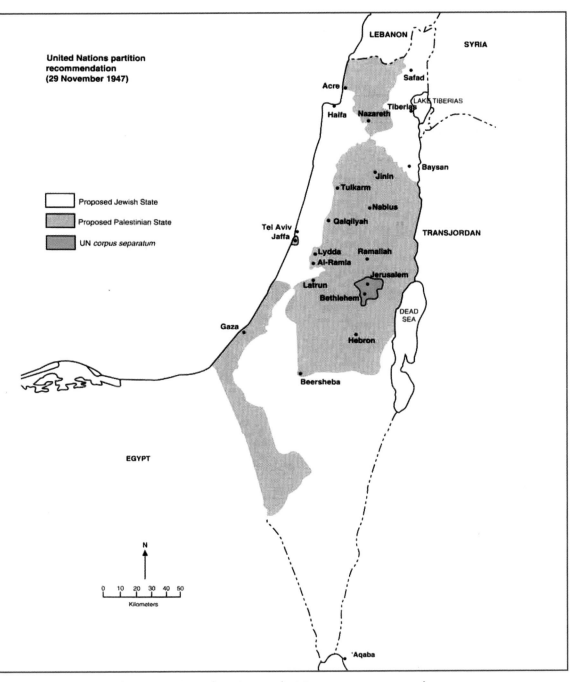

United Nations partition recommendation (29 November 1947)

LEBANON

SYRIA

Safad

Acre

LAKE TIBERIAS

Tiberias

Haifa   Nazareth

Jinin

Baysan

Tulkarm

Nablus

Qalqilyah

Tel Aviv
Jaffa

TRANSJORDAN

Lydda   Ramallah
Al-Ramla

Jerusalem

Latrun

Bethlehem

DEAD
SEA

Gaza

Hebron

Beersheba

EGYPT

Proposed Jewish State

Proposed Palestinian State

UN *corpus separatum*

N

0 10 20 30 40 50
Kilometers

'Aqaba

In November 1947, the United Nations presented a map to describe how the partition of Palestine would look. The UN took into account where the largest populations of Palestinian Arabs already lived in order to do its best not to displace people from their homes.

Historians still debate about the conquered lands. It is also a part of today's conflict between Arafat and the Israeli government. Because of the war, land that was going to become part of a Palestinian state became, instead, part of Israel. The debate ever since has been whether conquered lands should belong to Israel or become a Palestinian state. Since Israel began controlling the areas, thousands of Jews and others (including Arabs from elsewhere) have built new homes and towns there.

More than 500,000 Arab Muslims fell under Israeli rule in 1949. Many Palestinian Arabs left their land to avoid becoming part of the Israeli state. Many left because the Arab Muslim societies in the region began to break down. Arab communities began fighting each other over what to do and whom to support.

Arabs also left because they feared being killed. Israeli terrorist military groups such as Lehi and Irgun were attacking Arab communities. They attacked the village of Deir Yassin. Many Arab Muslim civilians were killed. The Israeli government said that it did not support the bombing in Deir

■ The last of the British troops leave Haifa, Palestine, in 1948. The British departure gave the Israelis control of the port city. Many Arabs fled Haifa, fearing Israeli rule.

Who Counts as What

This photo shows Arab men playing cards in Israel in 1950.

During the troubled times under British rule, thousands of people crossed into and out of the region. They did so legally and illegally. Historians acknowledge that thousands of Jews from elsewhere came and settled as new Palestinians. What is often overlooked is that thousands of Arabs from elsewhere did the same. Recently, according to EretzYisroel.org, since 1993 more than 250,000 Arabs from elsewhere have settled in Israeli-controlled areas. With all this coming and going, deciding who was and is an authentic Palestinian is tricky business.

The United Nations came up with its own definition of a Palestinian: anyone who spent two years in British-mandated Palestine before 1948, and their children, are Palestinians, be they Arab, Jewish, or something else.

Yassin. Terrorist activities are not easy to prevent, so attacks continued.

Some of British-mandated Palestine was taken over by Arab states. Jordan took control of the western hills of Judea and Samaria. This area became known as the West Bank. Egypt took control of the southern seashore, an area called the Gaza Strip. Jordan and Egypt controlled these areas for nineteen years. During that time, no Jews were allowed into the areas to worship at Jewish sites. Oddly enough, while these areas were under Arab control, there was no effort made to establish a Palestinian state in either area.

News of the Arab defeat in Israel's War of Independence spread throughout the Arab world. The defeat was humiliating. Arab groups formed to support the Palestinian Arab refugees who fled during the fighting. Other groups formed with the intention of attacking Israel until it no longer existed. Yasser Arafat became involved with both kinds of groups. Eventually, both groups combined into one. They believed the hope of true Arab unity was dependent upon the destruction of Israel. Without Israel, the Arab Muslim nation would be united from the Atlantic Ocean to the Persian Gulf.

Arafat the Soldier

It is uncertain when Yasser Arafat really started his military career. Some believe that he started at a young age. The easygoing Yasser liked to form neighborhood kids into military-style groups. Yasser was always in command. It was as a child that Arafat probably came into contact with Abdel Kader el-Husseini

The Palestinian People

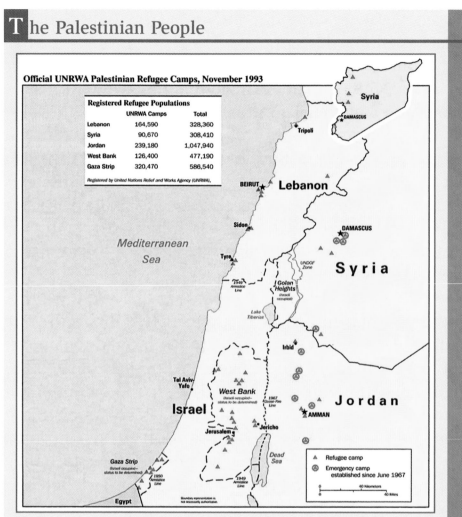

Official UNRWA Palestinian Refugee Camps, November 1993

Registered Refugee Populations

	UNRWA Camps	Total
Lebanon	164,590	328,360
Syria	90,670	308,410
Jordan	239,180	1,047,940
West Bank	126,400	477,190
Gaza Strip	320,470	586,540

Registered by United Nations Relief and Works Agency (UNRWA).

▲ Refugee camp

Ⓐ Emergency camp
established since June 1967

Palestinian refugees live in numerous camps within five separate areas.

During the 1800s and 1900s, "Palestinian" described all people living in the Holy Land, which included Jews, Muslims, and Christians.

It became popular to use "Palestinian" to describe Arab refugees during the 1930s and 1940s. Today, the media uses the word "Palestinian" to describe non-Jewish Arabs in Israel.

Israelis are the people living in the State of Israel. Most Israelis are Jews. There are also Arabs, Muslims, and Christians who are Israelis.

in Cairo. El-Husseini had set up the first organization of Palestinian students in Cairo. He used boys as carriers to buy guns and ammunition. The guns were smuggled into British-mandated Palestine for the Arab Muslim revolts of the 1930s. These smuggling operations continued right through Israel's War of Independence. By the end of 1947, Arafat, too, was helping in gun smuggling operations.

El-Husseini was killed in April 1948 in an Arab-Jewish conflict at Mount Kastel near Jerusalem. He was leading a local Palestinian-Arab army against Jewish groups. The news of el-Husseini's death shocked Arafat and his friends back in Cairo.

According to biographer Danny Rubinstein, the author of *The Mystery of Arafat*, Arafat and his friends met in a room of the Ikhwan al-Muslimun, or Ikhwan (Muslim Brotherhood). They burned their textbooks and student identification cards. They swore to go to Palestine to fight against the growing Jewish presence. They reached the border of Gaza sometime in May 1948.

This was just before the united Arab attack on Israel. Egyptian guards near Khan Yunis saw Arafat's group as misfit soldiers, so they took away their guns. The united Arab armies wanted to fight Israel with real military might, not with misfit military groups such as Arafat's. Arafat and his friends were sent away from the fighting. Arafat went to Jerusalem hoping to join the fighting there. Transjordanian soldiers turned Arafat away from there as well.

Arafat the Politician

Arafat temporarily gave up his hopes of fighting, but this event lasted in his memory. It upset him that the Arab army prevented him from fighting and that the army lost. It became obvious to Arafat that a Palestinian Arab was not allowed to fight for himself. Arafat believed that the united Arab army was a cruel traitor to Palestinian Arabs. He soon began saying that—above everything—he was a Palestinian. He was not necessarily an Arab, nor an Arab Muslim, but a Palestinian. This point of view was quite different from pan-Arabism, which many Arabs were backing.

Arafat returned to the University of Cairo and joined the Palestinian Students' League. Arafat continued his association with the Muslim Brotherhood, or Ikhwan. This was a movement founded in 1928 by Sheikh Hassan al-Banna. The Ikhwan was strongly against British control in mandated lands. It carried out violent revolts and riots against the British in Egypt. It also supported the Palestinian-Arab revolts in British-mandated Palestine during the 1930s.

Arafat says that he was a full-blown member of the Ikhwan from very early on and that he fought against the British in the Suez zone in 1951 during his third year of college. Ikhwan-related agents, such as Hassan Doh, have said that Arafat was not involved in the fighting at that time. Hassan Doh was in charge of military instruction in Egyptian universities. He trained Arafat, who was an excellent soldier in training. Arafat met physical demands very easily. He learned about guns and explosives. Within a month, Arafat became an instructor.

According to Arafat in a 1989 interview with Andrew Gowers and Tony Walker in *Behind the Myth*, "I held the British as the main people responsible for the

Palestinian tragedy. We are under their mandate and instead of giving us independence we became refugees and stateless. Hence I found it was my duty to participate with the Egyptians against the British troops."

Rising Political Star

Within a year of joining the student league, Arafat was elected its chairman in 1952. He formed a tight partnership with Salah Khalaf, also known as Abu Iyad. The two brought a very clear message to the league: "We are Palestinians!"

Also during this time, Egypt underwent great change. Military officers overthrew King Farouk. An Egyptian army colonel named Gamal Abdel Nasser took control of the country. Nasser changed the political landscape of Egypt. Nasser was a strong believer in Arab unity. His government gave funding to groups such as the National Arab Movement.

In the meantime, Arafat was developing his political skills within the league. He made speeches and gathered support for the league. Bashir Barghouti was a fellow league member. He remembered that Arafat would cry at the same point in many of his speeches. It was after reading four lines from a poem about Palestine.

Public Image

Arafat was becoming known as a man of mystery and unpredictability. He worked hard on his image. He began doing things to get noticed. On January 12, 1953, Arafat and fellow league members met with Egyptian general Mohammed Naguib. Arafat gave General

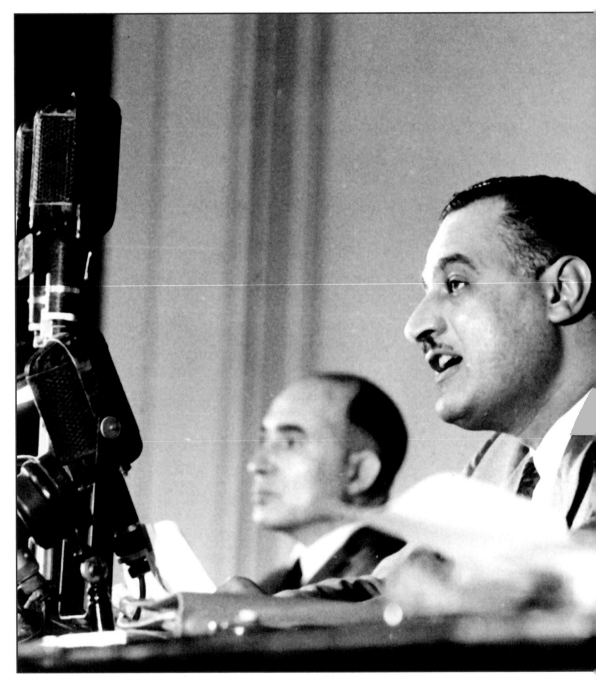

■ Gamal Abdel Nasser was a great inspiration to Arabs throughout the world. Many felt that Nasser's resoluteness was exactly what was needed to unite Arabs and combat foreign interference in the Middle East.

Naguib a petition. The signatures were signed in blood. The petition said, "Don't Forget Palestine."

Egypt was still a land of unrest, even with the new leader. There were many other leaders who wished to rule Egypt. In October 1954, Nasser was almost assassinated. He ordered a crackdown on all political movements other than government-supported groups. Arafat was arrested for being linked with the Ikhwan. He was freed a few months later.

In 1956, Nasser was elected president of Egypt. Nasser seized control of the Suez Canal, which was owned by France and Britain. Israel attacked Egypt with help from French and British forces. The war ended with an Israeli retreat. This was seen as a great political victory for the Arab world.

Pan-Arab movements began receiving funds and military aid from other countries, such as the Soviet Union. The United States feared this backing would bring more trouble to the Middle East. The United States decided to aid Israel.

Arafat served as an Egyptian soldier during the Suez Crisis (1956). He was a bomb disposal expert. When he returned to Cairo, he was hailed as a

Yasser Arafat

Profile of an Early Leader

Yasser Arafat walks alongside an aide in Beirut in 1982.

While others were getting degrees or getting married, Arafat focused on his league responsibilities. Fellow members have told many stories about Arafat's personality in the early days.

- Arafat was always moving, always working. He'd even do other members' tasks.

- Arafat didn't hide his feelings. If something upset him, everyone knew about it.

- Arafat made promises, even if he couldn't keep them. Often he made promises so that fellow Palestinian Arabs would feel confident in the league.

- Arafat often arrived late to meetings. His tardiness saved him from being arrested on many occasions.

- He rarely told people of his plans in advance.

hero who beat the mighty British and French. Even with the warm welcome, he believed it was time to leave Egypt. He completed his degree in engineering, then headed for Kuwait. Arafat secured a job at the Kuwait Public Works Department.

According to Arafat in an interview in *Behind the Myth*, "The interests of the Egyptians lost touch with the Palestinian movement, and became more involved in Arab Unity and pan-Arabism. After the Suez Canal War, Nasser began to move on the other side."

Palestinian Arabs were welcomed in Kuwait. Many enjoyed freedom and powerful positions. In 1958, Arafat and four friends got together to talk about the problems of the Palestine region. The friends were Salah Khalaf (from the students' league), Khalil al-Wazir, Farouk Kaddoumi, and Khaled al-Hassan.

The group met regularly to talk about the Arab powers and the Palestinian Arabs. They believed that the Arab states would never forcibly get the Palestinian region back from Israel. Soon, a few other friends joined. The young men decided to form a group to take action for the "liberation of Palestine."

Arafat's group was not a league, association, or political party. It was what Arafat hoped would become a movement. During a lively discussion, the group was named. They used the Arabic words for "Palestine Liberation Movement," which are *Harakat Tahrir Filastin*. They reversed the acronym and came up with *Fatah*, which means "conquest." Spelled forward the acronym is *Hataf*, which means "death." The group was thrilled. The name would be Fatah.

CHAPTER THREE
THE HOLY LAND

■ Above is a picture of Palestinian army recruits in 1940. Jews and Arabs both joined an Auxiliary Military Pioneer Corps to the British army.

While Arafat was growing up in Egypt, the Palestinian region was changing. Jews and Arab Muslims were fighting for control over the region. Jews and Muslims formed many small underground groups to fight against each other.

Many Arab Muslims and Jews claim rights to parts—or all—of Palestine. Many have claimed rights based on the history of Palestine. Both Jews and Arab Muslims have histories there. Arafat was aware of this from his first days in college. He learned how to use such claims to political advantage, starting with his work with the Palestinian Students' League and the Muslim Brotherhood.

The history of the Palestinian region is what makes it known as the Holy Land. Religion plays a major part in the war over Palestine. Both Jews and Muslims have holy shrines, or places of worship, throughout the region, especially in Jerusalem. Both groups feel they have a right to the land related to their places of worship.

Palestine was never a state, country, or power. Palestine was never a kingdom. There has never been a Palestinian language. Many people of different races and religions have lived in the Palestinian region. There has never been a separate ethnic race of people called Palestinians.

Ancient People and Religion

The Palestinian region is considered holy to Christians, Jews, and Muslims. Yasser Arafat is a Muslim. Judaism and Christianity began in Palestine. Jerusalem, an ancient city of Palestine, is considered the holiest place to Jews and Christians. Muslims consider it the third holiest place. The first two holiest places of Islam are Mecca and Medina (in present-day Saudi Arabia). Islam began in Mecca. Both Arab Muslims and Jews claim rights to control Jerusalem and the region.

Hebrews and Judaism

Ancient Jerusalem was built by the Semites in 2500 BC. Semites were ancient people related to Arabs, Hebrews, and Assyrians. The Palestinian region was known as Canaan. Between 1800 and 1500 BC, Hebrews settled into the region. They came from Mesopotamia (now Iraq) and developed communities. Eventually, the Hebrews outnumbered the other people living there.

Hebrews became known as Israelites. This name comes from the grandson of Abraham. Abraham is believed to be the father of the Jewish people. Abraham lived sometime between 1800 and 1500 BC. He had sons with two different women. One woman gave birth to a son named Isaac. Isaac fathered a son named Jacob. Jacob became known as Israel, which means "soldier of God."

Philistines settled in the region around 1050 BC. Philistines were from Asia Minor, which lies between the Mediterranean and the Black Seas. They were powerful and took over a lot of land in a short period. The Israelites fought the Philistines under the command of a man named David. He reduced the Philistines' territory to a narrow strip in southern Palestine. The Israelites made David their king around 1005 BC.

King David united the Hebrew tribes and other people in the region under one rule. He formed the Kingdom of Israel. He made Jerusalem the holy capital. David's son Solomon became king in 973 BC. He built important shrines, including King Solomon's Temple. It included what is today the Wailing Wall, which Arafat's relatives lived next to nearly a thousand years later.

Palestine's Name

The above painting depicts a victorious young David near the head of his adversary, Goliath.

The word "Palestine" comes from the Greco-Roman word *Palestina*. *Palestina* comes from the ancient word *Peleshet*. *Peleshet* means "Philistine." *Palestina* means "the Philistine country." The Philistines were not Hebrews or Arabs. They fought against the Hebrews (Israelites) over land in the Palestinian region.

The Kingdom of Israel included land on both sides of the Jordan River. Around 933 BC, the kingdom split in two. People in the north didn't want to support the cost of building Jerusalem, which was in the south. The northerners were also more liberal than the southerners. They were less strict in their religious practices. Israel became the kingdom in the north. Judah became the kingdom in the south. The word "Jew" comes from Judah.

The Kingdom of Israel was conquered by the Assyrians around 722 BC. Assyrians demolished the civilizations that they conquered. They destroyed the important buildings in Israel. They scattered all the people living there. The Kingdom of Israel—and its people—vanished.

The Kingdom of Judah was conquered by the Babylonians in 586 BC. King Solomon's Temple was destroyed. Many Judeans were sent to Babylon as slaves. They returned when Persia took control of the region in 539 BC. The temple was rebuilt. Greece took control of the region in 332 BC. Rome conquered the region in 63 BC. The temple was again destroyed. The Romans named the conquered region Palestina. Many Jews believed that this was done to crush them. It cut them off from their past. It made the history of the Philistines more tied to the land than the Jewish history. Palestina eventually became Palestine. Under harsh Roman rule, many Jews left the region for other lands.

Christianity

Jesus Christ was born in Bethlehem (near Jerusalem) between 6 and 4 BC. He was a Jew who challenged strict Jewish practices and customs. Still, some Jews chose to

Shared Roots

Gerbrand van den Eeckhout's *The Expulsion of Hagar*, 1666

Muslims also trace their roots to Abraham. Muslims believe that they are related to Abraham through one of his sons, Ishmael (Isma'il). Jews believe that they are related through another son named Isaac.

Two women gave birth to Abraham's sons. They were his wife, Sarah, and his servant, Hagar. Hagar gave birth to Ishmael. Sarah asked Abraham to send Hagar and Ishmael away. Muslims believe that Hagar and Ishmael went to Mecca. They found a sacred well there that kept them alive. Muslims believe that Abraham visited them later and built the Ka'bah in the Great Mosque of Mecca as a temple to Allah.

follow his teachings. Those who followed him became known as Christians. This was the start of Christianity.

Jews believe that Jesus was a normal man. They do not believe that he was the son of God or the messiah as Christians do. Muslims believe that Jesus was a prophet. Jesus traveled all throughout the Palestinian region to spread his teachings. Christians believe that he performed many miracles.

Islam

During ancient Palestinian history, the Arabs lived in Arabia (now Saudi Arabia). Powers such as Rome left the region alone because it was a vast desert. Arabs worshiped many gods. Like many ancient cultures, most Arabs lived in wandering tribes. During the AD 500s, busy trade routes formed through Arabia. Great towns grew to manage and direct trade and travelers. Mecca—an ancient town—blossomed with new trade.

The Ka'bah is in Mecca. It is a small shrine within the Great Mosque that holds the sacred stone. It is believed that this stone was sent from heaven. Many Arabian tribes and clans

■ Hundreds of thousands of reverent Muslims from all over the world make a pilgrimage to Mecca during Ramadan, a religious holiday that commemorates the revealing of the Koran to the prophet Muhammad. Pictured here is Mecca's Grand Mosque where the Ka'bah rock is located.

■ This eighteenth-century painting depicts the prophet Muhammad receiving the word of Allah during a battle. Muhammad went on to write down the words of the voices that he heard. Those words became the Koran, the Muslim holy book.

traveled to Mecca to worship the stone. Each tribe had different beliefs, which included worshiping different gods. Even with different gods, most tribes worshiped the stone. Most Arabs also believed that above all gods there was one with supreme power. That god was Allah.

The prophet of Islam, Muhammad, was born in Mecca about AD 570. In 610, he heard the voice of heaven, which told him to worship only Allah. He continued to hear the voice, which commanded him to accept the role of prophet. He told the people of Mecca to stop worshiping many gods.

The people of Mecca were not ready to worship only one god. They were not ready to stop worshiping the sacred stone either. The people in another town called Yathrib invited Muhammad to move there. He left Mecca for Yathrib in 622. Arabs who believed in his words followed him.

Muhammad became the ruler of the town. He changed the name of Yathrib to Medina. Medina means "the city of the prophet." He combined religious practices with political practices. He was a religious leader and a political ruler. Medina is the second holiest place to Muslims.

Muhammad wanted to seek vengeance upon the people of Mecca who did not listen to him. When groups of people left Mecca to travel, Muhammad and his followers attacked them. According to author Syed Asad Gilani, who wrote *Islam: A Mission, a Movement*, there were eighty-two battles. Muhammad led twenty-eight of them himself. Gilani believes that there was very little bloodshed in the battles led by Muhammad. In 630, he and his followers returned to conquer Mecca. The people

Muhammad's Trip

The prophet Muhammad (AD 570–632)

The trip, or pilgrimage, that Muhammad took to Yathrib is a sacred event. It is called *hirjah*. The trip marked the beginning of a powerful period in Arab history.

Most Muslims hope to make a pilgrimage to Mecca during their lifetime. It is to honor the birthplace of Muhammad. This trip is called the *hajj*. Millions of Muslims go during a specific time each year. Muslims who perform the hajj walk around the Ka'bah seven times. They try to kiss or touch the black stone located in the Ka'bah. Arafat performed the hajj in 1982 with his friend Khalil al-Wazir.

of Mecca agreed to worship only Allah. Muhammad decided to make the Ka'bah the main shrine of Islam.

Other Arabian tribes were impressed with Muhammad's taking over of Mecca. They converted to follow Muhammad. The religion was called Islam. "Islam" means "submission." Muslims become servants of Allah.

Muhammad was influenced by the monotheism of Judaism and Christianity. During Muhammad's time, Jews lived in Mecca and Medina. It is believed that Muhammad also knew many Christian beliefs. To Muslims, Allah is the same god as the Jewish and Christian god. Muslims believe that Abraham, Moses, and Jesus were prophets and that Muhammad is the last and greatest prophet. They believe that Allah gave his last instructions to Muhammad through the angel Gabriel. They believe these instructions take the place of any other instructions given to previous prophets, such as Moses.

Conquering Lands

Muhammad died only two years after ruling Mecca. Muhammad's followers continued with his religious and political practices. They developed the role of the caliph, which means "deputy of the prophet." This deputy served as the religious and political leader of the Muslims.

The first caliph was Abu Bakr. Under his rule (632–634), most other Arab tribes were conquered and converted. The Arab Muslim military moved out of Arabia and conquered neighboring lands. Around 640, the Arab Muslims conquered the Palestinian region.

The Dome of the Rock currently resides on a site that is sacred to Jews, Muslims, and Christians. Jews believe it to be the former location of Solomon's Temple, Christians find the area significant in relation to its connection with Jesus Christ, and Muslims believe the rock is the point from which Muhammad made his ascent into heaven.

They did not have a name for the region, so they used the Greco-Roman name Palestina.

By 711, the empire reached all the way to Spain. In less than a hundred years, the Arab Muslims had conquered all of Persia and most of the Roman territories. They became an incredible force in the world within a very short time.

Under Arab Muslim Rule

The Arabs did not insist that conquered people become Muslim. They planned to keep their religious identity apart from conquered peoples. They mostly wanted to be rulers and gather taxes. The Arab Muslims did, however, build many monuments to Islam in conquered lands.

In 691, a new shrine, the Dome of the Rock, was built over the former site of King Solomon's Temple. Arab Muslims claimed that Muhammad had stopped there on his journey to heaven.

Many people in the Palestinian region converted to Islam. They learned the Arabic language. The caliph ruled over them from his capital. The capital was first in Damascus, then later in Baghdad.

Religious Texts

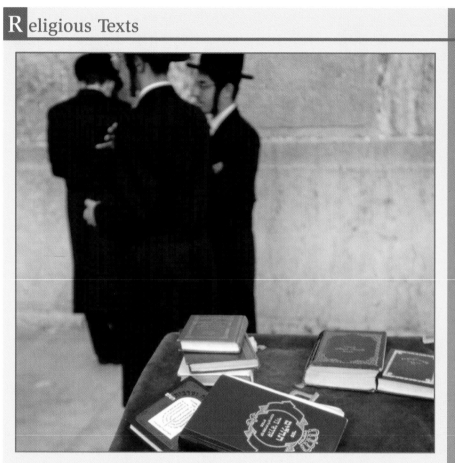

Jewish men gather at the Wailing Wall in Jerusalem in 1997.

Islam, Christianity, and Judaism share beliefs from the Bible. The story of Abraham comes from the Bible.

The Old Testament is the Jewish Bible. It is also called the Hebrew Bible or Tanakh. The Old Testament tells the story of Creation. It also explains the history of ancient Israel.

The Old Testament is the first part of the Christian Bible. The second part is the New Testament. It tells the story of Jesus Christ and the following years.

Muslims follow the Koran. Muhammad's followers copied Allah's instructions. The instructions were given to Muhammad from the angel Gabriel. The instructions became the Koran.

Turkish Muslim Rule

During the 1400s and 1500s, the Ottoman Empire took over the Arab Muslim lands. The Ottoman Turks were mostly Muslims. The Turks were accepting of other cultures and religions. Ottoman subjects were allowed to practice their own religions, such as Judaism and Christianity. Each religious group had its own community. The community was called a millet. A spiritual leader was elected to lead the millet. Each leader also reported to Ottoman officials.

During the late 1800s, many Jews built settlements in the region. They worked hard to change the dry, empty land into farming communities. Most of the rural people at that time were Arab peasants (Christian and Muslim). Large groups of Arab Christians and Jews were living in cities such as Nazareth, Jerusalem, and Hebron. The Ottoman Empire lasted until 1918. According to the *Columbia Encyclopedia*, in 1919, there were about 568,000 Muslims, 74,000 Christians, and 58,000 Jews in Palestine. When Britain took over the region, it became known as British-mandated Palestine.

Arafat and Fatah

No political or religious history was lost on Arafat. He understood its importance to any Palestinian statehood movement. Likewise, he knew that most people in the region would see that the symbolism and double meaning of Fatah/Hataf—conquest and death—was fitting for such a struggle. Arafat and his group embarked on altering the course of Middle East history.

CHAPTER FOUR
TRIUMPH AND TRAGEDY

■ Pictured above is Arafat speaking to a local magazine reporter during an interview in Beirut in 1980. He is wearing a fur cap that bears the emblem of Fatah, a faction of the Palestine Liberation Organization. Fatah merged with the PLO in 1968.

Fatah began publishing a magazine called *Filastinuna: Nida Al Hayat*, which means "Our Palestine: The Call of Life." The magazine had sketches, photographs, and poems. The first issue addressed the right of the "Palestinian" to return to his homeland. The Palestinian that this regarded was the Arab Muslim.

Most of the articles did not have an author's name attached. There were a few articles, which had "Y. A." as the author. In one such article, a photograph of a destroyed Palestinian Arab house was shown. The caption beneath read, "Houses destroyed as a result of the planning of the Arab League in 1948." This was basically saying that Palestinian Arabs were suffering because of the pan-Arab movement and the failed attack on Israel.

Fatah tried to remain secretive. Arab governments did not like independent Palestinian parties or organizations. The governments were trying to make the Palestinian cause a part of their own system. Independent organizations were too unpredictable and often had their own rules.

Fatah was very careful in recruiting new members. Each potential member was interviewed and had to take the following oath:

> I swear by God the Almighty,
> I swear by my honor and my conviction,
> I swear that I will be truly devoted to Palestine,
> That I will work actively for the liberation of Palestine,
> That I will do everything that lies within my capabilities,
> That I will not give away Fatah's secrets
> That this is a voluntary oath, and God is my witness.

Each member adopted a new name for the fight. Arafat became Abu Ammar. The name comes from a legendary Muslim warrior under Muhammad. The warrior was Ammar bin Yasser. Arafat's friend, Khalil al-Wazir, took the name Abu Jihad. *Jihad* means "holy struggle" or "holy war."

In order to get money for the movement, Arafat started working in the evenings on his own. He worked at the public works during the day and freelanced at night. Arafat told many people that his private work made him a millionaire. Many sources believe that Arafat exaggerated his success to show his importance in the business world.

During the early 1960s, Arafat made many trips to different cities. He recruited others for the movement. Everywhere he went he spoke of the Palestinian identity. He convinced others that the Palestinian people (Palestinian Arab refugees) needed to return "home." In order to do so, they would need to fight against Israel, Zionism, and anything standing in the way. Arafat wanted to challenge everything: Israel, the Arab states, and any Arab rulers who abandoned the Palestinians in previous years. He saw these rulers as traitors.

■ Arab refugees make their way toward Lebanon, fleeing the fighting going on in the Galilee region during the Arab-Israeli War in 1948. They are in northern Israel, what was then Palestine.

Arafat and his movement were getting a reputation among Arab leaders. Arafat began making demands that the leaders not get involved in Palestinian affairs. He took it upon himself to act as the official leader of Palestinian affairs. He left no doubt that he was "Mr. Palestine."

Fatah also began asking Muslim religious leaders to declare Fatah's "armed struggle" as a jihad. This would allow Arabs and Arab Muslims to see the attacks on Israel as something done for Allah. This also meant that any practicing Muslim would take the armed struggle seriously as a part of his or her worship to Allah.

The Fire Within

Egypt would again play a role in Arafat's life. Egypt established its own Palestinian movement in 1964. It helped establish the Palestine Liberation Organization (PLO). Arafat's Fatah organization was not involved in forming the PLO.

Arafat saw the PLO as a fake organization on the part of the Arab powers. It was another way for the states to talk about doing something without actually doing anything. Still, the establishment of another Palestinian movement caused Arafat to jump into action. Fatah made the decision to take military action against Israel.

Fatah's first attempts at its "armed struggle" against Israel failed. One of these attempts included an explosive charge that didn't explode. Israeli officials even found a trail leading from the failed explosive to the Jordanian border. The first Fatah member who died

The Man Behind the Glasses

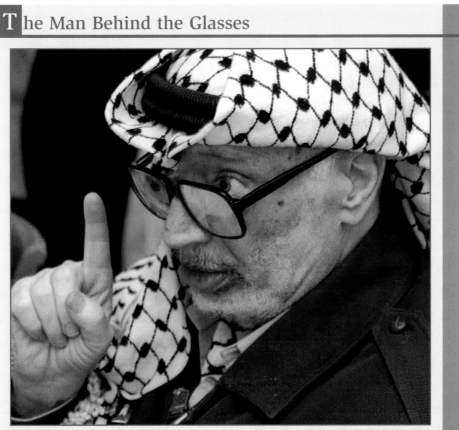

Arafat speaks to the Palestinian Legislative Council in Ramallah in 2002.

"Arafat is extremely careful about his 'careless' appearance," said Arafat's assistant to biographer Danny Rubinstein. Arafat's slouchy appearance is not a result of his being a messy guy. Arafat's appearance is carefully crafted. While other world leaders are clean-shaven and fancily dressed, Arafat is unshaven and wears casual clothes. Arafat looks like this on purpose. He wants to look like an average Palestinian Arab.

One of Arafat's must-wear pieces is his *kaffiyeh*. This is the large white scarf often seen wrapped about his head and dangling on one side. The part of the scarf dangling down is supposed to look like the shape of the Palestinian region. He began wearing it in 1956.

was not even killed by an Israeli. Ahmed Musa was killed by a Jordanian soldier. When he was crossing the Jordanian border after attempting to plant bombs in Israel, Jordanian soldiers stopped him. He refused to throw down his gun, so they shot him.

Even from these events, Fatah found ways to turn tragedies into triumphs. Arafat's gift of exaggeration helped. Word spread throughout the region about brave guerrilla fighters and martyrs. The very first announcement of Fatah's armed struggle was grossly exaggerated. It read: "Storm troops moved into the conquered territory in order to open the struggle against the enemy." It went on to say that hundreds of enemy soldiers were killed, even though that didn't really happen. Fatah used these announcements to get people talking.

President Nasser directed his spokespersons to speak against Fatah. He did not want Fatah to become a true competitor of the PLO. Egyptian spokespeople said that Fatah was a part of the Muslim Brotherhood, Ikhwan. Spokespersons said that Ikhwan received funds from the CIA (Central Intelligence Agency of the United States). They claimed that Zionist powers were getting Fatah to attack Israel. This, in turn, would allow Israel to attack its Arab neighbors, especially Egypt.

These insults did not harm Fatah; they actually gave the young group strength. Funds began pouring in from supporters, rich and poor alike. The Saudi government began supplying arms to Fatah. Soon other groups formed military branches to fight against Israel. These other groups claimed to represent Palestinian interests. The majority of Palestinians did not want war. They

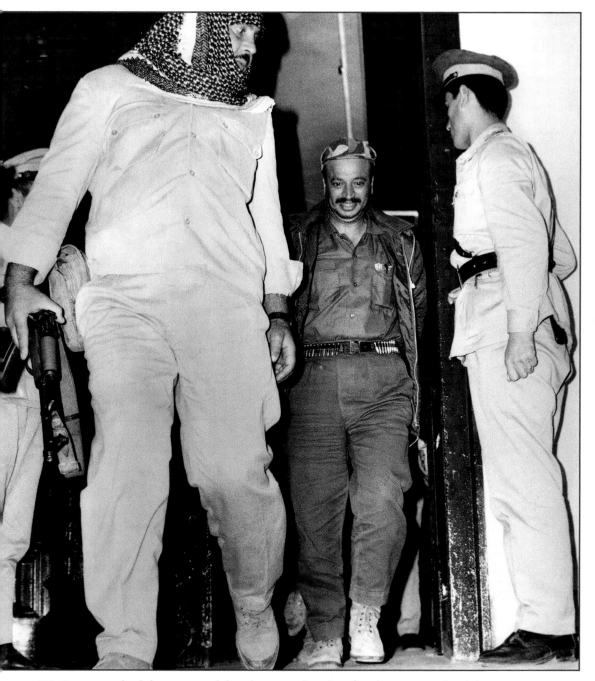

■ Surrounded by armed bodyguards, Arafat leaves a building in Damascus to attend a press conference in 1969. Arafat had recently come to an agreement with the Lebanese army about permitting some actions against Israel.

Yasser Arafat

Arafat at a ceremony in Cairo after observing forty days of mourning for the Egyptian president, Gamal Abdel Nasser, in 1970

Arafat was arrested by the Syrian and Lebanese governments during his rise to power. He was arrested in Syria on charges that he was attempting to explode an American oil pipeline. He was also arrested in connection with two murders of Fatah members. While in jail this second time, he went on a hunger strike. He collapsed on the thirteenth day.

When he was arrested in Lebanon, he pretended to be someone else. The officials questioned him for two months. They finally let him go, believing that he was a Syrian soldier. Later they realized that they had captured and released the guerrilla fighter Yasser Arafat.

wanted what they claimed had been taken from them: their lands and freedom.

Tension was mounting within Fatah. It had grown into a complex organization. Fellow members began to form different opinions about Fatah and Arafat as its military commander. In 1966, the central committee suspended Arafat from his command duty. Charges included that he spent money unwisely and sent false military reports to make defeats look like victories, especially in the battlefield.

Arab Muslim terrorist groups formed at the borders of Israel. In May 1967, President Nasser stopped Israeli ships from using the Gulf of Aqaba. Egypt sought agreements with neighboring Arab countries. In June, Syria, Jordan, and Iraq agreed to form a joint military command.

Israel knew what was coming—another united Arab attack. On June 5, 1967, Israel launched a surprise attack on Egypt. Iraq, Jordan, and Syria went to the defense of Egypt. Facing the Arab nations, the Israeli forces were ready to defend Israel.

The war ended on June 10. Arabs call it the June War while Israelis call it the Six-Day War. Israel defeated the Arab powers in borderlands that were once a part of the Palestinian region. Israel took control of the Sinai Peninsula, the West Bank, Gaza, East Jerusalem, and the Golan Heights. Israel again had expanded its territory. The Israeli government said that it would return some of the territory to Arab control under certain conditions. While Israel calls the lands "administered areas," others call them "occupied territories."

■ Arafat speaks with Egyptian president Gamal Abdel Nasser at a 1969 meeting in Cairo. Nasser was a crucial mediator between Lebanese and Palestinian interests. The day before he died, Nasser organized a meeting between Middle East leaders in an attempt to put an end to the conflict.

The Six-Day War was once again humiliating to Arabs. Arafat and Fatah were not involved in the fight, and therefore not connected with the humiliation that the Arab armies faced. Toward the end of 1967, PLO members suggested that Arafat be invited to join. They did so because while the Arab unity failed, Fatah was finally having great success.

Fatah's mission against Israel continued after the Six-Day War ended. Fatah members carried out raids from Palestinian Arab refugee camps along the Jordan River. They planted mines and threw grenades. Targets were any Israeli—soldier or civilian. On March 18, 1968, an Israeli school bus hit a mine. A schoolboy and an adult were killed. Twenty-nine children were injured.

Israeli leaders were furious. Arafat and Salah Khalaf were called away from the refugee camps to meet with the commander of the Jordanian army. He warned them that Israeli troops would be coming to demolish Fatah and other anti-Israeli groups. He suggested that Arafat flee to the nearby hills. Arafat refused, wanting to meet the "Israeli enemy" head on.

On March 21, Israeli tanks crossed the border into Jordan. The Jordanian army was told not to fight against Israel, but some units joined in anyway with scattered terrorist forces. The Israeli army broke from its war plan, which caused confusion. Thirty-four Israeli tanks were hit. The Israelis withdrew.

Victory

Arafat—and the Arab world—saw this as a great victory. He said it was "the first victory for our Arab nation after the 1967 war." In saying this, he was uniting his Palestinian cause with something he constantly criticized, which was the Arab world. Without help from the Jordanian army, Fatah would have been crushed. This fact didn't matter to Arafat. He needed recognition for Fatah. He needed average Palestinians to believe in Fatah's work for their nationalist cause. The victory became known as Fatah's victory. Muslim religious leaders set up funds for the jihad.

Arafat was elected Fatah's spokesperson. Before long, Arafat's photograph was everywhere. Newspapers and magazines couldn't get enough of the mysterious leader. He invited news cameras to film nighttime raids. *Time* magazine put a photograph of Arafat on its cover. His movement was named "the powerful new force in the Middle East."

Opportunity Knocks

In April 1968, Nasser agreed to meet with Arafat. Nasser promised to give guns and training to Arafat's men, which he did. He took Arafat with him on a trip to Moscow, where Arafat received Soviet funds for his cause.

Members of Fatah are shown raising their arms in surrender. King Hussein's firm resolve helped stop the fighting. Relations between Jordanians and Palestinians have been historically shaky.

While Arafat was enjoying growing fame, his fellow Fatah members were changing their political ideas. Some began to believe that an Arab-Jewish state could be created using the entire ancient Palestinian region. Such a move could be achieved through peaceful means. This separation is what the UN agreement of 1947 had sought. The Israelis had agreed to this at the time. Jews and Arabs would live side by side as equals. This was just one of many ideas that greatly differed from Arafat's. Arafat wanted all of the old British-mandated Palestine to be an Arab Muslim state.

Arafat's Private Life

Raymonda Tawil, mother of Suha Arafat, at her home in Ramallah in 1999

While the private lives of leaders are often known, Arafat's has remained a secret. When asked what he does in his spare time, he says that he has no spare time. When asked whom he loves, he says he is married to Palestine.

While Arafat has been secretive, the world has seen enough through newspapers and interviews to find that he has a wife and child, and enjoys watching cartoons.

Arafat's wife:
- Suha Tawil, born 1963, Jerusalem
- Met Arafat around 1987
- Married Arafat in Tunis in 1990
- Her family is Christian
- Her father is a West Bank banker
- Her mother is a political activist/media star/PLO associate
- Wrote *My Life with Arafat* (in Arabic), 1993
- Gave birth to a baby girl in July 1995, named her Zawah after Arafat's mother

Fatah joined part of the PLO in July 1968. It joined the PLO's law-making body, which is the Palestinian National Council (PNC). Arafat had a very short wait to rise to power within the PLO. In February 1969, Arafat was elected the chairman of the executive committee of the entire PLO. Once again, Arafat's qualities made his peers put him into power.

The PLO

The Palestine Liberation Organization is as interesting as Arafat himself. It seems only fitting that Arafat would be the man to help it do impossible things. It was a governing body without a land on which to govern. It made important decisions about its people, who were scattered all throughout the Middle East and Europe.

Leadership of the PLO was not easy. The PLO was made of many different groups. These groups oftentimes clashed in their beliefs. Some groups wanted the liberation of the entire Palestinian region, including Israel. Some groups wanted a Palestinian state alongside Israel. Some wanted to wage war on Arab leaders who were considered traitors, such as Jordanian king Hussein bin Talal. This was particularly tricky since the PLO headquarters were in Jordan.

The PLO was allowed to operate in Jordan so long as it did not interfere with the Jordanian government. The PLO and all its parties waged attacks on Israel. Some attacks grabbed worldwide attention. The United States and other powers began to put pressure on Arab leaders. They wanted to build peace in the Middle East and stop terrorist attacks. Israel was not going to go away, no matter how many terrorists tried to destroy it.

A young Palestinian refugee takes up a rifle at a refugee camp. The refugee camp gave its support to the mission of Fatah and the PLO. Even women and young children did what they could to help Palestine's cause.

The rest of the world considered it to be a permanent nation.

Arafat and the PLO would not be deterred. In a 1970 interview with Italian journalist Oriana Falluci, Arafat is quoted as saying, "We shall never stop until we can go back home and Israel is destroyed . . . revolutionary violence is the only means for the liberation of the land of our forefathers . . . peace for us means Israel's destruction and nothing else."

On July 23, 1970, President Nasser accepted an American peace plan. Fatah attacked Nasser's decision on its radio station, which Nasser swiftly shut down. Before the end of the year, Nasser died of a heart attack.

King Hussein of Jordan met with Israeli leaders in secret in 1970. He promised to prevent terrorist actions against Israel. He began to crack down on terrorist activities based in Jordan, including those by the PLO. In August 1970, terrorist attacks were directed at King Hussein. The Jordanian army then attacked PLO headquarters. Arafat begged other Arab leaders to come to his assistance. Some PLO groups were carrying out actions without Arafat's permission. The forty-year-old Arafat

■ In this photo, Arafat is shown attending the funeral of Egyptian president Gamal Nasser. The economic aid Nasser gave to Arafat's PLO did not buy Arafat's constant allegiance. Arafat used Fatah and other PLO groups to criticize Nasser's policies with the West.

was furious, but he could do very little to get the giant PLO movement under control.

War broke out between PLO groups and the Jordanian army. The war became known as Black September. Thousands of Palestinian Arab refugees were killed. Arafat and the PLO moved to Lebanon and Syria. They were shaken but not rid of their spirit.

"If you strike the movement in their last hold-outs, I'll follow you to the end of the earth, to my dying breath, to give you the punishment you deserve" was Salah Khalaf's warning to King Hussein in 1971.

Black September

The Black September organization terrorized the Middle East with attacks for nearly three years (1971–1974). The group assassinated Jordan's prime minister, Wasof Tel, on September 28, 1971. Arafat denied knowing of the group or working with them. Many experts believe Arafat in fact did set up Black September to do the violent work that he did not want the PLO to be involved in.

On September 5, 1972, Black September attacked the Israeli Olympic team headquarters in Munich's Olympic Village. Munich was hosting the Summer Olympic Games. German police handled negotiations with the terrorists. The attack ended with the murders of all the Israeli hostages.

Arafat again avoided claiming responsibility. Many experts today believe Arafat did not order the attack. It was also clear, though, that Arafat could not fully control the splinter groups he had set up. These people were increasing their violence. The violence did not

■ Munich's chief of police, Manfred Schreiber, checks his watch while negotiating with one of the terrorists *(far right)* who took Israelis hostage at the 1972 Olympics. In 1999, Abu Daoud, the ringleader of the 1972 massacre, published an autobiography entitled *Memoirs of a Palestinian Terrorist*, admitting the PLO's connection to the incident.

bother Arafat, but he did not want terrorism connected to the PLO. This was a trying time for Arafat. To many, he became a hated villain with a murderous cause. Israeli prime minister Golda Meir immediately set up a team to work against terrorism. The main targets were PLO group leaders and terrorist leaders. Arafat avoided getting killed, but many other targets did not. The PLO continued actions against Israel.

CHAPTER FIVE

LEADER OF TODAY AND TOMORROW

■ While at the 16th National Palestinian Council in Algiers, Arafat visited a military training camp near Tebessa. Here, he is teaching Palestinian forces methods of attack using a bayonet.

In 1970 Anwar Sadat replaced Nasser as Egyptian president. Sadat urged Arafat and the PLO to break away from terrorist activities. He suggested that they form a government in exile. This government would use means other than an "armed struggle" to achieve a Palestinian state. A government in exile could set up diplomatic relations with the United Nations. By working peacefully, such a government would get much more support from countries worldwide.

In 1973, Palestinian Arabs in the West Bank wrote letters to the UN. They asked the UN to pressure Israel into releasing control of the West Bank and the Gaza Strip. They asked for a mini-state in the areas called Palestine. Arafat's Palestinians were taking a new path, excluding him from the negotiations. Arafat sent the West Bank Palestinian Arabs a message stating that the PLO supported them.

Nonetheless, attacks continued between PLO groups and Israelis. President Sadat planned a war to end the attacks. Egyptian and Syrian armies would attack Israel once again. The attack was not to destroy Israel as previous wars were. It was to get into a position that would put Arabs on equal footing with Israelis. He hoped they would all eventually participate in peace talks. With all parties being equal, there was more of a chance to bargain for a Palestinian state.

The Yom Kippur War

On October 6, 1973, Arab armies attacked Israel. Arafat wasn't told about the attack until the evening before. Israel was unprepared because it was the Jewish holiday, Yom Kippur. The war is known as the Yom Kippur War and the October War. Arab armies made limited advances into Israeli territory. After three weeks of fighting, the armies accepted a cease-fire.

Questions surfaced among Arafat's movement. Should they try another way of getting a Palestinian

Many lost their lives in the Yom Kippur War. The Israelis were preoccupied observing the holiday and were caught off guard by the attack. Yom Kippur, the Jewish day of atonement, is the most sacred holiday in Judaism and is sometimes referred to as "the Sabbath of Sabbaths."

state? Was it possible to get a Palestinian state by finally recognizing Israel's right to exist? These questions divided the PLO. Some extreme groups left the PLO because they strongly believed that Israel needed to be destroyed. They believed that the PLO would be dragged down the path to peace with Israel. Even the Palestinian Arab refugees were divided on what to do.

Despite the coming peace talks, the PLO decided in June 1974 to continue the armed struggle against Israel. It wrote the Phased Plan. This plan stated that getting a mini-state by "any means" would help to accomplish the long-term goal. "Any means" meant other ways in addition to an armed struggle. The long-term goal was getting back all of Palestine. Sources differ on whether "all of Palestine" actually meant the eventual destruction of Israel. In October 1974, the Arab nations chose the PLO as the official representative of the Palestinian Arabs.

An Olive Branch and a Gun

In 1974, the UN General Assembly set time aside for a discussion about

Palestine. More than 115 countries voted to allow the PLO to join the discussion. These countries were sympathetic toward the "underdog" that the PLO publicized itself as being. Among those countries voting against this move included the United States, Bolivia, the Dominican Republic, and Israel.

New York City (the UN host) spent more than $750,000 to protect Arafat on his visit of less than twenty-four hours to the UN. Extreme Jewish groups were promising to kill Arafat before he left the city. Tens of thousands of demonstrators gathered in front of the UN, shouting, "Arafat, go home!"

Arafat addressed the General Assembly. He described himself as the son of Jerusalem. He compared himself to George Washington and Abraham Lincoln. He spoke of a Jewish invasion of Palestine. The speech was his opportunity to give his history of a people called Palestinians to the world.

Arafat knew the world was now listening. As the voice of the Palestinian people, he took advantage to outline their struggle. He clearly defined Israeli Zionism as the enemy

■ Arafat argues the case of Palestinians to the world in what would become one of the most famous speeches given at the United Nations. Heads of Arab states accepted the PLO as the representative of all Palestinians.

of Palestinians' hope to create their own homeland, or to even share the land:

> It pains our people greatly to witness the propagation of the myth that its homeland was a desert until it was made to bloom by the toil of foreign settlers, that it was a land without a people, and that the colonialist entity caused no harm to any human being. No: such lies must be exposed from this rostrum, for the world must know that Palestine was the cradle of the most ancient cultures and civilizations. Its Arab people were engaged in farming and building, spreading culture throughout the land for thousands of years, setting an example in the practice of freedom of worship, acting as faithful guardians of the holy places of all religions.
>
> As a son of Jerusalem, I treasure for myself and my people beautiful memories and vivid images of the religious brotherhood that was the hallmark of Our Holy City before it succumbed to catastrophe. Our people continued to pursue this enlightened policy until the establishment of the State of Israel and their dispersion. This did not deter our people from pursuing their humanitarian role on Palestinian soil. Nor will they permit their land to become a launching pad for aggression or a racist camp predicated on the destruction of civilization, cultures, progress and peace.
>
> Our people cannot but maintain the heritage of their ancestors in resisting the invaders,

in assuming the privileged task of defending their native land, their Arab nationhood, their culture and civilization, and in safeguarding the cradle of monotheistic religion. We need only mention briefly some Israeli stands: its support of the Secret Army Organization in Algeria, its bolstering of the settler-colonialists in Africa—whether in the Congo Angola, Mozambique, Zimbabwe, Azania or South Africa—and its backing of South Vietnam against the Vietnamese revolution.

In addition, how can we not mention Israel's continuing support of imperialists and racists everywhere, its obstructionist stand in the Committee of Twenty-Four, its refusal to cast its vote in support of independence for the African States, and its opposition to the demands of many Asian, African and Latin American nations, and several other States in the conference on raw materials, population, the Law of the Sea, and food.

All these facts offer further proof of the character of the enemy which has usurped our land. They justify the honorable struggle which we are waging against it. As we defend a vision of the future, our enemy upholds the myths of the past. The enemy we face has a long record of hostility even towards the Jews themselves, for there is within the Zionist entity a built-in racism against Oriental Jews.

While we are vociferously condemning the massacres of Jews under Nazi rule, Zionist leadership appeared more interested at that time in exploiting them as best it could in order to realize its goal of immigration into Palestine. If the immigration of Jews to Palestine had had as its objective the goal of enabling them to live side by side with us, enjoying the same rights and assuring the same duties, we would have opened our doors to them, as far as our homeland's capacity for absorption permitted.

Arafat made a point to separate the "enemy," Zionism, with ordinary Jews. His words sought to distinguish just who and what the Palestine Liberation Organization fought for and against. He also defined for those listening just what was and was not terrorism:

[S]ince its inception, our revolution has not been motivated by racial or religious factors. Its target has never been the Jew, as a person, but racist Zionism and undisguised aggression. In this sense, ours is also a revolution for the Jew, as a human being, as well. We are struggling so that Jews, Christians and Muslims may live in equality, enjoying the same rights and assuming the same duties, free from racial or religious discrimination.

We do distinguish between Judaism and Zionism. While we maintain our opposition to the colonialist Zionist movement, we respect the Jewish faith. Today, almost one century after the rise of the Zionist movement, we wish to warn of its increasing danger to the Jews of

A Confusing Plan

View of the Old City, Jerusalem, 1972

UN Resolution 242 is a plan that has been understood in many different ways. Its wording has led Arabs to believe that Israel should withdraw from all territories it has ever conquered. Others, including people who helped write it, say it means something else.

UN Resolution 242 "calls on the parties to make peace and allows Israel to administer the territories it occupied in 1967 until 'a just and lasting peace in the Middle East' is achieved. When such a peace is made, Israel is required to withdraw its armed forces 'from territories' it occupied during the Six-Day War—not from 'the' territories nor from 'all' the territories, but from some of the territories," according to Eugene Rostow, undersecretary of state for political affairs from 1966 to 1969.

the world, to our Arab people and to world peace and security. For Zionism encourages the Jew to emigrate out of his homeland and grants him an artificially created nationality. The Zionists proceed with their terrorist activities even though these have proved ineffective. The phenomenon of constant emigration from Israel, which is bound to grow as the bastions of colonialism and racism in the world fall, is an example of the inevitability of the failure of such activities.

We urge the people and governments of the world to stand firm against Zionist attempts at encouraging world Jewry to emigrate from their countries and to usurp our land. We urge them as well firmly to oppose any discrimination against any human being, as to religion, race, or color.

Why should our Arab Palestinian people pay the price of such discrimination in the world? Why should our people be responsible for the problems of Jewish immigration, if such problems exist in the minds of some people? Why do not the supporters of these problems open their own countries, which can absorb and help these immigrants?

Those who call us terrorists wish to prevent world public opinion from discovering the truth about us and from seeing the justice on our faces. They seek to hide the terrorism and tyranny of their acts, and our own posture of self-defense.

The difference between the revolutionary and the terrorist lies in the reason for which each fights. For whoever stands by a just cause and fights for the freedom and liberation of his land from the invaders, the settlers and the colonialists, cannot possibly be called terrorist, otherwise the American people in their struggle for liberation from the British colonialists would have been terrorists; the European resistance against the Nazis would be terrorism, the struggle of the Asian, African and Latin American peoples would also be terrorism, and many of you who are in this Assembly hall were considered terrorists.

This is actually a just and proper struggle consecrated by the United Nations Charter and by the Universal Declaration of Human Rights. As to those who fight against the just causes, those who wage war to occupy, colonize and oppress other people, those are the terrorists. Those are the people whose actions should be condemned, who should be called war criminals: for the justice of the cause determines the right to struggle.

Arafat knew how to make his words and meaning memorable, and he spoke these words to conclude his speech: "Today, I have come bearing an olive branch and a freedom fighter's gun. Do not let the olive branch fall from my hand."

Arafat was speaking symbolically. He was warning that he could be peaceful or violent depending on the reaction to the Palestinian Arab problem. He was urging the UN to help him be peaceful. Arafat did indeed have a gun holster in his jacket. He left his gun backstage.

On November 22, the General Assembly voted to allow the PLO to attend UN activities on a permanent basis. Arafat's victory at the UN brought in millions of dollars for the PLO. Nonetheless, it continued its attacks on Israel. At the same time, some PLO members began campaigning for peace. Said Hammami, the PLO representative in London, begged Israeli Jews and Palestinian Arabs to recognize each other as equals. Israeli leaders were seeing a new side of the PLO. Up until then, they saw it as a terrorist organization. A few lower-level leaders on both sides began holding secret meetings.

Changing Times

President Sadat signed a peace treaty with Israel during the Camp David Accords. Arafat had sent Sadat a letter pleading with him not to sign it. In doing so, Sadat was the first Arab power to recognize Israel's right to exist. This made him very unpopular among Arab Muslims. In October 1981, members of his own army assassinated Sadat. Arafat believed the same thing could happen to him if he made a deal with Israel.

In the treaty, Israel agreed to give back the Sinai Desert (which is three times the size of Israel). Israel honored its promise. This began a new relationship between Arab powers and Israel. It was a relationship of negotiation. It showed that Israel was willing to let go of occupied territories or administered areas under certain conditions.

■ Arafat addresses the UN General Assembly in Geneva, Switzerland, in 1988. The United States had denied Arafat a visa to come to New York, so the General Assembly agreed to meet in Switzerland.

What's at Stake

The United Nations Security Council votes to approve a resolution to demand a cease-fire in the Middle East in 2002.

For a Palestinian state to be fully established in Gaza and the West Bank, a set of conditions detailed by both sides need to be met. Israel and the Palestinian Authority have to meet each other's desires.

- The Palestinian Authority (PA) wants to name and control Jerusalem (all of it) as its capital. Jerusalem has been the Israeli capital for decades. Neither can agree.
- The PA wants Israel to tear down all Jewish settlements in the administered areas. The settlements are home to Jewish civilians who have worked to build up the areas. Israel does not want to tear them down. Neither can agree.
- The PA must stop all terrorist activities before it can establish the Palestinian state. As recent as 2003, the PLO has possibly been linked to terrorist activities.

Hearing Voices

Those who wanted a Palestinian state in Gaza and the West Bank could not be silenced. Arafat found a new struggle and a new movement. It was the struggle to get Israel to withdraw from the West Bank and Gaza

UN Resolution 242 of 1967 supported this action. It also said that there needed to be a lasting peace in the region. The plan called for the recognition of Israel by all parties. Parties also had to end all acts of terrorism. UN Resolution 242 was the basis for most of the Middle East peace talks.

For years, Arafat and the PLO rejected Resolution 242. King Hussein of Jordan tried several times to get Arafat to agree to the conditions of the resolution. Hussein wanted a Palestinian state in the West Bank, which would be linked to Jordan. Often the meetings ended with King Hussein in a furious fit, shouting his frustrations about Arafat and his stubbornness. In 1988, King Hussein gave up his ties to the West Bank and to negotiating with Arafat.

Arafat realized that now only he could speak to the world about getting a Palestinian state. He also knew that he would need to accept UN Resolution 242 and other plans that wouldn't sit well with Arab Muslims. Beginning in August, he flew to many Arab countries in order to speak with Arab leaders. Arafat intended to accept the plan as long as the United States and other powers would accept Palestine's right to rule itself.

On December 14, 1988, in Geneva, Switzerland, Arafat did what many thought impossible. He announced to the world that he and the PLO accepted Israel's right to exist. He said that the PLO would totally

S tumbling Blocks to Peace

While leaders were working toward peace, violence erupted throughout Israel:

Arafat embraces Iraqi president Saddam Hussein *(right)* in 1980.

- 1987—Four Palestinians are killed in a traffic accident. Palestinians in administered areas launch the intifada, which means "uprising." Riots and attacks against Israeli soldiers occur. PLO is linked to the intifada.
- 1988—Khalil al-Wazir, Arafat's longtime friend is assassinated in Tunis, the capital of Tunisia. Israel is blamed.
- 1989—Large numbers of Jews from Russia begin settling in occupied territories/administered areas. Riots and revolts occur.
- 1990—Iraq invades Kuwait. Arafat publicly supports Iraq's leader Saddam Hussein, who is anti-Israel and anti–United States.
- 1991—Salah Khalaf, Arafat's longtime friend is assassinated in Tunis.
- 2000—Another intifada is launched in the administered areas. Hundreds of Israelis and 1,800 Palestinian Arabs are killed.

stop further use of terrorism. The United States agreed to resume peace talks with the PLO.

Golden Years

Although Arafat was entering the age when most people retire, he was raring to go. The next decade would challenge whether he really wanted peace and a Palestinian state. Today he is still in the process of proving this to Israel and the world.

The road to peace was not easy—and it is still being paved. Arafat was a representative of the Palestinian cause. There were many different opinions about the cause and its future. There were—and are—groups acting through terrorism on behalf of the Palestinian Arab cause. Part of Arafat's work would be to stop these groups.

Arafat has used his political skills to make everyone believe that a Palestinian state was coming soon. He smooth-talked until people with completely opposing ideas trusted him. Whether he was talking to extreme terrorists or to world leaders, he focused on the long-term goal. It didn't mean that Arafat was away from his terrorist past. According to CBS's *60 Minutes*, the PLO has remained connected to some terrorist groups.

Secret Peace

Israeli government leaders and Arafat's assistants began secret peace meetings in 1993 in Oslo, Norway. This led to an agreement. Palestinians would be granted self-governance in the Gaza Strip. They would also get self-governance in Jericho, a town in the West Bank. This would be a test to see how peacefully a Palestinian state could exist next to Israel.

Later, in Washington, D.C., Arafat met with Israeli prime minister Yitzhak Rabin. The two leaders signed the agreement. Further allowances of land would be given to the Palestinian people in the administered areas (occupied territories) over time. Many Arabs were outraged by Arafat's peace agreement. In 1994, the Islamic jihad led by Dr. Fathi Shkaki made a statement that it was perfectly all right to assassinate Arafat.

After twenty-five years away from the Gaza Strip, Arafat returned there in July 1994. He established the first Palestinian government. It is called the Palestinian Authority (PA). The PA was to establish new laws and services for the Palestinian people. It was to help govern the Palestinian people while respecting Israel. Israeli military would be present but would slowly withdraw until peace was achieved.

In December 1994, Arafat and two Israelis shared a global honor. He was awarded the Nobel Peace Prize. Yitzhak Rabin and Israeli foreign minister Shimon Peres shared it with him. Soon after, Yitzhak Rabin was assassinated. He was killed by a Jewish citizen who was angered by the peace agreement. Saddened greatly by the news, Arafat told *Time* magazine, "I lost my partner."

President Arafat

On January 20, 1996, the first Palestinian elections were held. Arafat won more than 85 percent of the vote. He became president of the Palestinian Authority. Arafat busied himself with the details of establishing the Palestinian government.

Even today as the PA is setting up government systems in Gaza and the West Bank, there are still old issues

Mahmoud Abbas accepted the position of PLO prime minister in March 2003. His knowledge of PLO politics was supposed to help him negotiate a peace between Israel and the PLO.

to negotiate. One issue is the disagreement over controlling Jerusalem. It has been Israel's capital for many years. The PA plans to make Jerusalem its capital as well.

On October 23, 1998, Arafat made another agreement with Israel. He and Prime Minister Benjamin Netanyahu met at Wye River, Maryland. They agreed on more rules to help firmly establish the Palestinian state in the West Bank. Even during peace talks and under peace conditions, terrorist activities were carried out.

In July 2000, Arafat met with the new Israeli prime minister, Ehud Barak, at Camp David in Maryland. For the first time, the Israeli government was willing to discuss Jerusalem. Arafat didn't like some of the conditions, so he walked out of the peace talks.

In February 2001, Ariel Sharon became prime minister of Israel. Sharon's dislike of Arafat is world famous. By the end of 2001, the Israeli government cut off ties to Arafat. This was done because Arafat had not proved he was stopping terrorist attacks against Israel.

"I don't know anyone who has as much civilian Jewish blood on his hands as Arafat since the Nazis' time," Sharon said in October 1995.

The Israeli government decided to isolate Arafat in Ramallah. Starting on February 6, 2002, he was not allowed to leave. Whether the West Bank and Gaza would become an independent, peaceful Palestinian state was yet to be seen.

More terrorist attacks occurred during 2002, which prompted Israeli tanks to storm Arafat's compound in March. In May, Arafat walked out of his compound to the cheers of fellow Palestinians. They chanted, "God is great."

In June 2002, a Palestinian Arab suicide bomber killed more Israelis. Again, Arafat's Ramallah compound

■ At a rally commemorating the thirty-sixth anniversary of Fatah, a young Fatah supporter stands beside a portrait of Yasser Arafat on December 31, 2000. Later, high-profile Israelis and Palestinians were killed in separate ambushes.

The Arab World

Around 90 percent of all Arabs are Muslims. Countries or states that make up the Arab world have Arab governments.

The Arab world includes eighteen countries:

- Algeria
- Bahrain
- Egypt
- Iraq
- Jordan
- Kuwait
- Lebanon
- Libya
- Mauritania
- Morocco
- Oman
- Qatar
- Saudi Arabia
- Sudan
- Syria
- Tunisia
- United Arab Emirates
- Yemen

There are populations of non-Arabs living in Arab countries. They include the Kurds of Iraq and the Berbers of northern Africa. Many Arabs also live within non-Arab countries, such as Iran and Israel.

was stormed by Israeli troops. Eventually, President Arafat exited unharmed. He flashed a wide grin to the Palestinians, who again chanted, "God is great."

In 2003, the PA established another leadership position to work alongside President Arafat. It created the role of prime minister. Arafat nominated sixty-seven-year-old Mahmoud Abbas for the position.

Mahmoud Abbas was a founding member of Fatah. Born in Sufad, Palestine (now part of Israel), in 1935, Abbas was known as Abu Mazen for many years working inside the Fatah movement. Abbas gained his position as prime minister through international approval after Arafat's presidency was accused of obstructing the peace process. In June 2003, Abbas threatened to resign his post as prime minister. He demanded that the PLO Central Committee outline how to move forward with confidence-building steps as outlined in the United States's Roadmap to Peace initiative outlined in June 2002. Arafat and the Central Committee refused Abbas's resignation. They vowed to help him work with Israel so the peace process would not be delayed further.

The working relationship between Abbas and the Central Committee did not improve, however. Abbas did not have control of all PLO security services. The most vital, perhaps, remained in the grasp of Arafat. Abbas's frustrations boiled over in September, and he sent a letter of resignation to Arafat. On September 6, Arafat accepted Abbas's resignation.

Arafat offered the prime minister position to longtime PLO colleague and PA parliament speaker Ahmed Qorei. Qorei told a group of international reporters, as recorded by CNN: "I'm looking from the Americans, from the Europeans, from the quartet, for a real support—practical, not by words. I want to change the situation on the ground for the Palestinian people." Qorei accepted the nomination on September 10. The United States and Israel reacted positively, but with caution. Both countries said they would work with Qorei and the PLO if he would fight terrorism and fulfill obligations to the Roadmap initiative.

While tensions are still high between Israel and the PA, there are hopes that peace talks will continue. Peace will be reached only when Israelis and Palestinians feel safe. Arafat, who is in his seventies, believes that he may see an independent Palestinian state as soon as 2005. The nation of Palestine may become a reality in his golden years.

TIMELINE

1929 Yasser Arafat is born Mohammed Abdel-Raouf Arafat al-Qudwa al-Husseini on August 4, 1929, in Cairo, Egypt.

1933 Arafat's mother dies of kidney failure. Arafat and his younger brother, Fathi, are sent to Old City, Jerusalem, to live with an uncle.

1937 Arafat and his brother return to Cairo to live with their newly remarried father and stepmother. During his school years in Cairo, Arafat earns the nickname "Yasser," meaning "easy-going," from neighborhood friends.

1948 Arafat graduates from high school in Cairo and enrolls in a civil engineering program at King Fouad I University in Cairo.

1952 Arafat joins the Muslim Brotherhood and Palestinian Students' League. Within a year, he is elected Students' League chairman.

1953 Arafat and other league members meet with Egyptian general Mohammed Naguib to deliver a petition for the Palestinian cause.

1956 Arafat serves as an Egyptian soldier during the Suez Crisis as a bomb disposal expert.

1957 Arafat forms Fatah with a group of friends. Fatah begins attacks on Israel.

1966 Fatah Central Committee suspends Arafat from his command duty.

1968 Arafat meets with Egyptian president Gamal Nasser in April to ask for aid to Fatah. In July, Fatah becomes part of the Palestine Liberation Organization (PLO).

1969	Arafat is elected chairman of the PLO's executive committee.
1972	The Black September group, connected to the PLO, murders Israeli athletes during the Munich Olympic Games.
1974	Arafat addresses the United Nations in New York City.
1982	Arafat and the PLO move headquarters from Lebanon to Tunisia.
1988	In November, the Palestine National Council (PNC) announces Palestinian independence according to UN Partition Plan 181. In December, Arafat speaks for the PLO and accepts Israel's right to exist.
1993	Secret peace meetings between the Israeli government and the PLO lead to the Oslo agreement and the "land for peace" policy.
1994	Arafat returns to Gaza after a twenty-five-year absence. He establishes the Palestinian Authority (PA) to oversee the governing of new territories. In December, Arafat shares the Nobel Peace Prize with Israeli president Yitzhak Rabin and Israeli foreign minister Shimon Peres.
1996	The first Palestinian public elections are held and Arafat wins more than 85 percent of the vote to become the first president of the Palestinian Authority.
1998	Arafat and Israeli prime minister Benjamin Netanyahu agree on the Wye River

Memorandum defining further control of occupied territories by the Palestinian Authority.

1999 Arafat and Peres meet for continued peace talks.

2000 Arafat and Israeli prime minister Ehud Barak meet at Camp David, Maryland, to discuss PA rule of Jerusalem. Israel is willing to give up more land and control to the PA than ever before. Arafat walks out of talks with no agreement when some conditions are not met.

2001 Ariel Sharon is elected new Israeli prime minister.

2002 Arafat is refused travel outside Ramallah in the West Bank by Israel. The Israeli army enforces the isolation. In June, United States president George W. Bush presents the "roadmap to peace" that will reopen talks between Israel and the Palestinian Authority.

2003 Arafat and the PLO executive committee establish a prime minister position to head the peace negotiations. Mahmoud Abbas, a longtime associate of Arafat's, accepts the position but resigns after six months. Arafat nominates Ahmed Qorei to replace Abbas.

ally A person or country that gives support to another.

assassinate To murder someone.

caliph Deputy of the prophet Muhammad; religious and political leader of the Muslim people.

civilian Someone who is not a member of the armed forces.

civilization A highly developed and organized society.

conflict A serious disagreement; a war or period of fighting.

conquer To defeat and take control of an enemy.

declaration The act of announcing something, or the announcement that is made.

endorse To support or approve of someone or something.

exile To send someone away from his or her own country and order the person not to return.

exterminate To kill large numbers of people, animals, or insects.

immigrate To come from abroad or live permanently in a country other than one's birthplace.

interrogate To question someone in detail.

intifada Arabic for "shaking off"; a term used for staging an uprising.

isolate To keep something or someone separate.

jihad A holy war.

Ka'bah A shrine in the Great Mosque in Mecca, containing the sacred stone of Islam.

majority More than half of a group of people or things.

mandated territories Areas of land controlled by another power until self government can be established.

martyr Someone who is killed or made to suffer because of his or her beliefs.

messiah Savior.

monotheism The belief in one god.

mosque A building used by Muslims for worship.

Mukata Arafat's compound in Ramallah.

negotiation Bargaining or discussion of something so that parties come to an agreement.

Palestine Name of region between Egypt, Jordan, and Syria before British partition in 1937.

pan-Arabism The belief in a united Arab nation under one rule.

petition A letter signed by many people asking those in power to change a policy or action, or telling them how the signers feel about a certain issue or situation.

politics The debate and activity involved in governing a country; the activities of politicians and political parties; or an individual's beliefs about how the government should be run.

prophet A person who speaks words given directly from God.

refugee A person who has to leave his or her home because of safety, war, persecution, or disaster.

sacred Holy, or to do with religion; deserving great respect.

shrine A holy building that often contains sacred objects, or a place that is honored for its history or because it is connected to something important.

terrorist Someone who uses violence and threats to frighten people into obeying for political ends.

Zionism A movement to build a Jewish national state in British-mandated Palestine, which is considered the ancient Jewish homeland.

Americans for Middle East Understanding
475 Riverside Drive, Room 245
New York, NY 10115-0245
(212) 870-2053

The Arab Organization for Human Rights (AOHR)
91, Al-Marghany Street
Heliopolis
Cairo, Egypt
e-mail: aohr@link.com.eg
Web site: http://www.aohronline.org

The Middle East Institute
1761 North Street NW
Washington, DC 20036-2882
(202) 785-1141

The Palestine Liberation Organization
Negotiations Affairs Department
Attn: Director General
P.O. Box 4120
Al-Bireh, Ramallah, Palestine
Web site: http://www.nad-plo.org

Zionist Organization of America
4 East 34th Street
New York, NY 10016
(212) 481-1500
e-mail: info@zoa.org
Web site: http://www.zoa.org

Web Sites

Due to the changing nature of Internet links, the Rosen Publishing Group, Inc., has developed an online list of Web sites related to the subject of this book. This site is updated regularly. Please use this link to access the list:

http://www.rosenlinks.com/mel/yara

Ferber, Elizabeth. *Yasir Arafat: A Life of War and Peace*. Brookfield, CT: Millbrook Press, 1995.

Grossman, Laurie. *Children of Israel*. Minneapolis: Lerner Publishing, 2000.

Jamieson, Alison. *Terrorism*. New York: Steck-Vaughn, 1995.

Nuweihed, Jamal Sleem, and C. Tingley (translator). *Abu Jmeel's Daughter and Other Stories: Arab Folk Tales from Palestine and Lebanon*. Northampton, MA: Interlink Publishing, 2001.

Reische, Diana L. *Arafat and the Palestine Liberation Organization*. Danbury, CT: Franklin Watts, 1991.

BIBLIOGRAPHY

Alexander, Yonah. *The Role of Communications in the Middle East Conflict—Ideological and Religious Aspects*. New York: Praeger Publishers, 1973.

Buber, Martin. *Israel and Palestine—The History of an Idea*. London: Horovitz Publishing Company, Ltd., 1952.

Buber, Martin. *On Zion—The History of an Idea*. New York: Horovitz Publishing Company, Ltd., 1973.

Canaan, T. *The Palestinian Cause*. Jerusalem: The Modern Press, 1936.

Gilani, Syed Asad. *Islam: A Mission, a Movement*. Lahore, Pakistan: Islamic Publications Ltd., 1982.

Gowers, Andrew, and Tony Walker. *Behind the Myth—Yasser Arafat and the Palestinian Revolution*. London: W. H. Allen, 1990.

Heller, Joseph. *The Zionist Idea*. New York: Schocken Books, 1949.

Kaysi, Marwan Ibrahim al-. *Morals and Manners in Islam—A Guide to Islamic Adab*. Leicester, UK: The Islamic Foundation, 1986.

Ralph, Philip Lee, Robert E. Lerner, Standish Meacham, and Edward McNall Burns. *World Civilizations—Their History and Their Culture*. New York: W. W. Norton & Company Inc., 1995.

Rubinstein, Danny. *The Mystery of Arafat*. South
   Royalton, VT: Steerforth Press, 1995.
Steuart-Erskine, Beatrice. *Palestine of the Arabs*.
   London: George G. Harrap & Co., Ltd., 1935.

About the Author

Bernadette Brexel is a journalist and author with an avid interest in political science.

Photo Credits

Front cover map courtesy of the Library of Congress; front cover image, pp. 1, 3 (chapter 3 box), 43, 44, 57, 93, 95 © Corbis; pp. 3 (chapter 1 box), 10, 21, 25, 26, 32, 36, 39, 46, 70 © Hulton/Archive/Getty Images; pp. 3 (chapter 2 box), 19, 23, 28 © Perry-Castãnedia Library Map Collection/The University of Texas at Austin; pp. 3 (chapter 4 box), 52 © Hussein Jarikji/AP/Wide World Photos; pp. 3 (chapter 5 box), 4, 6, 55, 66, 72, 83, 87 © AP/Wide World Photos; p. 8 © Adel Hana/AP/Wide World Photos; pp. 15, 34, 59, 62, 79, 90 © Bettmann/Corbis; p. 41 © North Carolina Museum of Art/Corbis; p. 48 © Hanan Isachar/Corbis; p. 50 © Nik Wheeler/Corbis; p. 60 © Gulio Broglio/AP/Wide World Photos; pp. 65, 76 © David Rubinger/AP/Wide World Photos; p. 68 © Owen Franker/AP/Wide World Photos; p. 74 © Alain Nogues/Corbis; p. 88 © Evan Schneider/AP/Wide World Photos.

Designer: Nelson Sá; **Editor:** Mark Beyer;
Photo Researcher: Nelson Sá